Hours of the Desert

Hours of the Desert

Poems by

Roxanne Doty

© 2024 Roxanne Doty. All rights reserved.
This material may not be reproduced in any form, published,
reprinted, recorded, performed, broadcast,
rewritten or redistributed without
the explicit permission of Roxanne Doty.
All such actions are strictly prohibited by law.

Cover design by Shay Culligan
Cover image by David Chorlton
Author photo by Don Laurence Photography

ISBN: 978-1-63980-519-8

Kelsay Books
502 South 1040 East, A-119
American Fork, Utah 84003
Kelsaybooks.com

My heartfelt thanks to the poets and other writers in the greater Phoenix area and beyond who listened to and read my work and provided so much support and encouragement.

Any profits from *Hours of the Desert* will be donated to Keys to Change (formerly Human Services Campus)
in Phoenix, Arizona
which encompasses over a dozen nonprofit organizations that serve people experiencing homelessness.

Acknowledgments

Thank you to the following publications, in which versions of these poems previously appeared, sometimes with different titles:

Avatar Review: "A Dive Bar Called the Bardo" (as "Coming Home New Year's Eve")

Espacio Fronterizo—Journal of Encounters: "Bare Life," "Eloy, Arizona," "Backpacks"

International Times: "Deliverance," "Hours of the Desert," "Dear Citizen"

The New Verse News: "Friday Night on East Van Buren," "Intolerance Degree Zero"

Ocotillo Review: "Grey Wolves," "A Sonoran Desert City"

Quibble Lit: "To the Wild"

Stride Magazine: "Backsplash"

Unstrung: "Honey Crisp"

Contents

The Border

Backpacks	15
Deliverance	16
Eloy, Arizona	17
Intolerance Degree Zero: A Letter From Homeland Security	18
The House in Arivaca	19
Hours of the Desert	20
The Bracelet	21
Vaya Con Dios	22
Dear Citizen	23
Sketcher High Tops	24
Crossing the Line	25
Border Security Tour	26
Angel of the Sonoran	27
Welcome to Texas	28
Bare Life	29
Eyes of the Desert	30

The City

Phoenix, 1976	33
A Time in the Desert	34
Dancing Man	35
Friday Night on East Van Buren	36
Blood Moon	37
Memorial Day at Starbucks	38
A Dive Bar Called the Bardo	39
Loretta Lynn in Central Phoenix	41
Exit 145A	42
Honey Crisps	43
A Sonoran Desert City	44

Backsplash	45
Lead Me Home	46
Morning Rush Hour at Southern and the 101/Price Freeway	47

The Land

To the Wild	51
Salvation	52
Heat	53
Gray Wolves	54
The Sonoran	55
Palm Fronds	56
Scorpions	57
Desert Columbine	58
Mountains	59

The Border

Backpacks

They surround us, barely noticed, sprawled on the floor of
classrooms, strung over the shoulders of students streaming
across campuses, seemingly insignificant containers of books,
lecture notes and pieces of knowledge, but some scatter on vast
and deadly desert floors, lay next to water bottles, hang from
Ironwoods and Mesquites in remote places, branches bending
under their weight, some empty, faded from the sun, ripped
at the seams, left behind, some with supplies like cans of tuna,
beans, a wallet, a pair of shoes, a love letter, photos of family,
holy cards with images of Jesus Christ, prayers printed
on the back that promise a quicker trip to heaven and if you
listen to the absences you might hear heartbeats around these
backpacks, your own and a sad symphony of pulses of those
who carried the packs, and I have tried to do this, to write
about these backpacks, feeling they were crucial to understand,
like the shoes piled high at the Holocaust Museum in D.C.
and I have always failed to come close enough to their silences.

Deliverance

(for the world's migrants)

If there be a god, may she grant you
a safe journey, the days quiet, nights gentle,
the earth beneath your feet firm, may the miles
melt, may the guides be fair, leave you unharmed,
if there be a god may she protect your children,
keep them near you, unscarred, may she bind
the tongues of border guards who demand
papers, for once may your flesh and heart suffice
to prove your worth, may politics sleep
for a thousand years as you cross, may the deserts
be kind, the seas calm.

May defeat not break your bones, destroy
your spirit, may the Ironwoods offer shelter,
the arms of Saguaros hold you if you fall,
may oceans carry you, may you arrive
with dignity, may documents fall from the sky
like soft rain into your hands, may you be met
with respect, may wisdom not die, may we reach
out our hands to you, may you not have to wait,
may you not be sent back, may your dreams
become our world.

Eloy, Arizona

The one-eyed woman in the laundromat looks at you
has no use for your sparkle
the academic glitter that sticks to you
like baubles and costume jewelry
mean nothing to her clothes spinning in the dryer,
the small change in her purse

Down the road sits the Eloy Detention Center
of course, she knows about it
everyone in this town of shuttered storefronts
knows about it, private prisons, the only businesses
that do not fall to the fierce sun and blowing dust
but she doesn't want to talk to you
sees right through you and your voyeuristic desire

The beds in the detention center are filled
with paperless people who know the tunnels
the desert's death traps
the walls and fences, the raids
the fragmenting of families
the violence of the law
the shadow world

The woman in the laundromat doesn't trust
your sterile sentences, your sanitized words
your theories and concepts
the comfort of your ordered spaces
the stories told in large conference rooms
with pitchers of ice water on long tables

She asks what right you have
to be in Eloy, Arizona
to stand before the swirls
of barbed wire that glisten in the heat
so easy for you
to walk away

Intolerance Degree Zero: A Letter From Homeland Security

Dear Migrants and Asylum Seekers,
We are implementing policies to keep our homeland
safe from your scattered bones and disobedient
dreams that traverse la linea between our air and yours.
We have executive orders, vacant Walmarts
and Bible verses on our side. In the name of sovereignty,
we will send vultures to swoop heavy over the hearts
of your children, seal loopholes in arid scratches of earth
with blood from blisters on your feet. We will erase
your name and bury your destiny in an open grave
on the migrant trail as we watch the sky rain dust
from skeletons of all the crossers we have funneled
into the killing fields of the Sonoran, Mohave
and Chihuahuan Deserts. And if you emerge
from these wastelands, we will warehouse your sons
and daughters behind the stripes of our flag,
as sludge spills from the sewers of our mouths.
God bless America, we are not a sanctuary,
we do not do body counts, and we do not keep track
of where we send your babies.

The House in Arivaca

A man left his port city of tourist beaches
and few jobs, walked along the edges
of towns, across expanses broken
by distance and belief, in sunrises
and sunsets, alone and for a time followed
by a Mexican gray wolf who also had travelled
far, muscles slick and strong, its tail pointed
towards the sky, it knew nothing of borders,
but sensed the danger of humans who hunt
and extinguish, wear intolerance
like a holstered weapon.

A helicopter whirled above, blades slashed
the air, whipped the dust, the man took shelter
in a dry arroyo, waited for it to leave
and when he raised his head, his eyes
met those of the gray wolf who understood
the loss of home and journeys of risk
the creature turned its long muzzle
toward an adobe house, which seemed to the man
a mirage of water quivering
in the sun's glare.

An old woman stood on a small porch,
a woman of justice and love, a story teller,
protector of the land and those who migrate
through it, she pointed to cans of tuna
and beans, bottles of water. The man folded
his hands in reverence and acknowledgement,
bowed. The woman did the same and he walked
back into the blue dusk of the desert.

Hours of the Desert

When the desert. When far from cities, but close. When
Ironwood Forest and Organ Pipe and Devil's Highway.
When a trail becomes a plea. Because the distance is long.
When as close to god as you'll ever get.
When still an illusion.

When layover spots. Because dreams. When abandoned
backpacks and love letters, books of poetry, books of prayer,
empty water bottles. When shade is a black plastic bag over
creosote and cactus. When the sun. When days are fire,
when snakes take cover.

When a bracelet on the ground. When someone wore it.
Because flesh and blood. Because someone wrote the love
letters, held the books of poetry and prayer. Because
a heartbeat.

When still the heat. When nothing but the heat.

When the future lies beyond mountains. When it disappears.
When a mirage of water. When a man with no features.
When he hides in a uniform. Behind a weapon. Inside the law.
When on your knees.

When grace. When compassion. When kindness.
When humanity. When lost.

When you walk again. When the dream and the prayer
and grace and the snake and the man cross the same desert
all unaware of each other. When over and over again.

When clusters of black dots mark places of death.
Because the bones. When white crosses. When no
identificado. When bodies don't get counted. When they do.
When counting doesn't matter. When justice is a moment.
Of madness. When it dies.

The Bracelet

A mile from Puerto Blanco Road in Organ Pipe National
Monument, down a vaguely-marked trail, past a cluster
of creosote bushes in a landscape of endless distance
devoid of meaningful markers, our truck out of sight,
summer air on the verge of erupting with heat, a bracelet
lays on the ground, the kind you see in little shops and on
racks of street vendors in dusty Mexican border towns,
religious scenes glued to small oval pieces of wood, sealed
in hard plastic; the Virgin Mary, Jesus on the cross, St. Francis,
the holy family shimmer on the desert floor next to a Humane
Borders water station, each scene separated by two silver beads
and strung together with a thin strip of elastic maybe here under
the hot sun for a long time or perhaps the bracelet recently
slipped from the wrist of a young woman thirsty from her long
journey to a hoped-for-better-life, as she turned the 55-gallon
barrel's spigot for a drink of water placed here by human beings
who do not concern themselves with documents or skin color
or different languages that flow from desperate lips and I pick
up the bracelet, hold it in my hand for a moment, hope the
water enabled the young woman to continue, hope she made it
to safety and later at home I place the bracelet in a box with
other objects I have found in the desert; a love letter, a soccer
card with a photo of a player named Ivan Cordoba, an empty
box of matches and a small booklet with the words, Human
Rights for the Migrants in Spanish, fragile connections, the
presence of these objects, the absence of those who lost them.

Vaya Con Dios

All they will call you will be deportees.
—Plane Wreck at Los Gatos by Woody Guthrie, 1948

I met Jose at the Douglas, AZ border patrol station, picked
up for crossing without papers. Along with other detainees
he would be bussed back across the border to Agua Prieta
later that afternoon. He had crossed five times already,
said he would cross again, probably the next day. He was
heading for Goshen, Indiana where his friend lived, hoped
to find work. We sat on a grey metal bench facing one
another, my tape recorder on a small table in front of us.
Jose's English was much better than my Spanish. Fifty-three
years old, wore thin wire-rimmed glasses, beige pants, a plaid
shirt. He reminded me of Eric Clapton. His dark eyes sparkled
when he smiled, which he did frequently. He said there was no
work in his home of Vera Cruz. He had a daughter who
attended university. I told him I had a daughter too. She would
start Arizona State University in the Fall. The interview was
too short. I wanted to walk out of the Douglas, Arizona Border
Patrol Station with Jose, find a cafe and talk some more. Have
a snack, maybe lunch. It was almost noon. I wanted to drop him
off at a bus station, no papers required. Send him on his way
to Goshen. I wanted all the arbitrary divisions between us
to explode, shatter into tiny particles of dust and disappear
in the heat of the surrounding desert. A guard came for Jose to
take him back to one of the rooms where they held detainees.
I remembered a phrase from a song my mom used to play
on our stereo when I was a kid, *Vaya Con Dios*. Back then,
I had no idea what those words meant but liked the way they
sounded. Like flying, like safety, like freedom. "Vaya Con
Dios," I said as Jose turned to leave with the guard.
I wanted to believe a god existed and would travel with him.
Jose smiled and we shook hands.

Dear Citizen

In your name, men on horseback in uniforms and Stetsons snap reins like whips, steer steeds along the banks of the Rio Grande, in pursuit of those who approach the shore carrying shoes, clothes, bags of food, babies above their heads, away from currents running through this river that once flowed freely but now struggles to reach its destination, human beings with names and stories who journeyed far through jungle, cities, countries, paid everything to reach this land of promise and merciless borders. Citizen, do you think your god would scar the earth with such ugly marks that must be traversed to arrive at a place of peace and human kindness only to be met by these men who drive them back? Citizen, is this what you want?

Do you believe the politician's anger roiling beneath calm words, proclamations this is not who *we* are? But, Citizen you must know this is precisely who *we* are, children have been taken, families broken, innocents detained, blind eyes turned, bodies strewn across our deserts, floating in the waters of the world, the men on horseback allowed, this latest cruelty shadowed by old cruelties, lingering cruelties shielded by words, justifications, policies that built the world, *our* identities, *their* identities, the *us*, the *them*, the *we*.
Citizen, this word that contains you has become tainted, stained, can no longer hold.

Prompted by photos in the *New York Times,* Sept. 21, 2021 of U.S. Border Patrol's treatment of Haitian migrants.

Sketcher High Tops

A man of the cloth, gun rack in his pickup
showed me the Ironwood Forest, trails
and layover spots, trees draped in black
plastic shields from the sun. Walk at night,
rest during the day. Bottles with water
or urine. Never waste fluids. He drew a map.
This is where they cross. Added clusters of red
dots. This is where they die. A photo
from his pocket. Prudencia Martin Gomez dead
from U.S. border policy, and the desert starkly
beautiful, reduces its victims with brutal celerity.
Eighteen years old. From Todos Santos, Guatemala.
Long, dark hair spread above her head
like a halo stretching across the sand,
stained with body fluids pooled on the ground
around this young girl, this child, this daughter
and the shoes still on her feet, black with white
soles and laces securely tied. Sketcher High Tops,
the same kind I bought my eighteen-year-old
daughter at Target. I imagined their legs sprawled
on the carpet in my family room watching TV,
a bowl of popcorn on the floor beside them.
Prudencia and my daughter next to one another,
wearing those shoes.

Dedicated to Rev. Dr. Robin Hoover who showed me the trails migrants travelled, the death traps they encountered and the water stations supplied by Humane Borders.

Crossing the Line

The person who trembles while crossing a border casts doubt on their own definition.
   —Helene Cixous, *Three Steps on the Ladder of Writing*

A boy wears a Scooby Doo sweatshirt, gazes at my camera,
a brother on either side, one holds a soccer ball, their feet dangle
from the concrete bench, shoe laces missing. The father nods
permission for the photo. Altar, Sonora has run out of shoe laces,
demand high for this dangerous item confiscated by Border Patrol.
No papers, no laces.

The father paces the plaza, passes us a slip of paper, *us* who cross
with ease, marvel at the beauty of the desert, the thrill of racing
through black, empty night, this magnificent land spread
before us like prayer, *us* who freely return to places we've left
temporarily, homes and families. *Us* with our children's
shoe laces tied securely.

White vans line the street. One will take them north to the border,
crammed with other travelers, seekers, an assortment of humanity.
It will be dark when they cross the line of cruelty and promise,
la frontera, divider between one place and the other place,
indistinguishable to the white-tailed deer, pronghorns, javelinas,
creatures who do not honor human markers of division.

"Tell her we're okay." The father nods at a scrap of paper
passed to us, a Tucson phone number, a woman's name.
"She's their mother. Tell her we're crossing tonight."

Border Security Tour

Scholars visit the Nogales, Arizona Border
Patrol Station, arrive with an arsenal
of facts, theories, concepts, names
of prominent thinkers carved on their souls,
so far from air-conditioned Hilton Hotel
conference rooms, elaborately choreographed
conversations still ringing in their ears,
they arrive at this shadow world and wait
like fair-goers in a shooting gallery
to try the *Pepperball Launching System*
aimed at a cardboard figure, substitute
for a human being, the acronym PLS
makes me think of the word please,
as in please don't use these weapons
you call non-lethal that discharge
ten pepperballs per second, release
a scent like baby powder when they hit
a target, i.e. a human being, but PLS
rolls off the tongue like a bullet
leaving the barrel of a gun, loaded
with power and purpose
as the border patrol agent explains targets
are blinded but only for a moment,
so, no worries though the scholars appear
slightly uncomfortable as the first in line
takes aim and fires.

Angel of the Sonoran

Boom box in her right hand she carries
music, records forgotten sounds
of dried bones whispers of lost spirits
names of the dead and the soft breath
of promise, left arm swings at her side
black hair flows like lava, her long skirt
grazes the earth, billows like hope
navigates hostile terrain beneath a pallid sky
scratched with faint drifts of white cloud
fearless of heat and scarcity this woman
young or old wanders open stretches
of desert scrub, barren moonscapes packed
dirt and rock through an inferno of truth
she searches for souls *sin papels* or permission,
this unexpected angel timeless, fierce.

Inspired by Graciela Iturbide's photo *Mujer Angel, 1979.*

Welcome to Texas

It's okay little girl, mija. We're removing
your shoelaces, we don't want you to run away,
get lost or hurt. Here's your new house. Yes
it is a tent, it's not so cold like that other place.
You won't need those shiny mylar blankets
and when it gets hot, there's air-conditioning.
Pretend you are camping. Have you ever gone
camping? Here is your bunk. And your workbook.
No, you don't have to go to school. In fact,
there is no school here. Think of it as summer break
or Christmas holiday. We need to take
your mother away for a little while.
I don't know how long. You can talk with her
on the phone. Sometime. Please don't share
your food with the other children. Or use nicknames.
Don't cry or touch another child.
There is no hugging allowed.

Bare Life

We did believe that geography would be an ally to us.
—Doris Meissner, Immigration and Naturalization Services
   Commissioner, 1993–2000

The Commissioner closed points of entry,
turned to the prophets of policy, their suits
hungry for order and control, eyes
on elections to come, they nodded
approval, certain the searing heat, hostile
terrain would provide a moral alibi
for suffering of others and when bodies
fell along the corridors of death traversing
the great stillness of the Southwest deserts,
they labelled them unintended, denied
complicity, transformed men, women,
children into bare life subject to violence
without retribution, their lives taken
without consequence, the Sonoran and Chihuahuan
rendered sprawling graveyards
of the newly dead, skeletons, fragments,
numbers vast and uncertain.
Now, we wait for the lips of leaders
to finally stop moving, for sanitized words
stacked high on the altars of security and fear
to be crushed by the sheer weight
of human conscious and empathy.
We wait.

Eyes of the Desert

Legislators cut the world in half,
stabbed sands with slats of steel,
parted Pacific waters, split
the Sonoran and Sky Islands, divided
wildlife sanctuaries and national parks.
Bighorn sheep and jaguars
could no longer migrate.
Machines scraped the earth raw
and the lips of leaders swelled
while people knelt before the wall
believing in their own blood,
how it flowed differently from others
across the borderlines.
Followers enshrined their faith
in concertina wire and no one dared
reach through to an extended hand.
The desert watched from both sides,
the sweep of sun and fall of dusk.
Distraught, by violations thrust upon it,
pylons penetrating its skin, ashamed
of any complicity, it asked the air
for forgiveness, studied the vehicles,
drones and weapons, the razor sharpness
strung like tinsel above its body
and when the uniforms came close,
stomped heavy boots on its dry soil,
the desert spoke.
"Is this what you have become?"
It whispered, then shouted,
but the uniforms moved quickly
on foot and in SUVs, with empty
purpose and orders from far away,
and no one heard. The desert tried again,
"Is this what you have become?"

The City

Phoenix, 1976

Leave the east coast
drive cross country
you've heard of alchemy
out west substances
and dry glitter the closeness
of hallucination and illicit prayer
exit Interstate 17
and wander into the desert
city no lines on your face
who cares if the teachings
of Don Juan are a hoax
you believe in the wisdom
of lizards
the power of the right spot
stars in the perimeter
you will find the sky

A Time in the Desert

Van Buren seemed as good a place as any to exit Interstate
17 on that warm December day all those years ago when I
wandered onto the border of a paradise where freedom blurred
with desperation and stark desolate beauty embraced the neon
city that promised and exhausted passions of pilgrims
gathered on this street in the sun, speaking words of wisdom
and plain bullshit, longing for original dimes long lost
in the shadows of a magic that could only happen in the presence
of mountains and Saguaro and illegal substances traded in shady
places under untrimmed palm trees and how could I have known
that the heart of this land and people would be sucked hollow
by private spaces of privilege and iron gates of security
and the magnificence that surrounded me would be replaced
with an eternity of red-tiled repetition blighting first the periphery
of my world and then the very center and that I would mourn
this desert whose powerful presence touched me one sunny
winter day when I stared it in the eye, no lines on my face,
no wisdom in my soul.

Dancing Man

He lifts one leg, then the other.
side-skips across concrete
at the Mill and Southern bus stop.
Cut-off denims, red jockey hat,
black knee-high socks
and green Sketchers.
Dancing man waves to passing cars,
like a celebrity to fans.

Tonight, he rides the 8:00pm eastbound,
winks at me as if we share a secret,
taps his feet and points to the Superstition
Mountains. *"That's the end of the line,"*
he says. The mountains are a dark mass,
the moon almost gold, looks like an egg
fallen on its side.

Friday Night on East Van Buren

It was the end of the line on Van Buren, a Friday night in April, a section of this gritty street where it leaves the city behind, disappears into east valley sprawl, and forgets the history that rumbles beneath its concrete and asphalt, the ghosts of old Phoenix that breathe the night air. The woman stood under the 202 overpass, moving from fence post to fence post, lightly touching each as if in a child's game or dance, her long hair flying in wind that rushed through the valley that night, blew dead palm fronds across the 4 lanes, debris into the air to flutter gracefully in the haze of dull streetlights and she walked into the oncoming traffic, stood with arms spread—a welcome or a plea or an effort simply to breathe and the cars stopped and watched and some blew their horns and waited as she got onto her knees and folded her hands in prayer in the glare of terrified headlights. And I wanted to say, leave her alone, give her space, don't call anyone, she has probably been fucked over time and again and beauty has a strangeness, and sadness a dignity and I looked around for red lights, for an official vehicle that might have been summoned. But the night remained still and free from authority and we waited and the woman finally rose, and walked to the other side of the street and climbed the incline toward the highway and the traffic began to move again.

Blood Moon

East-bound light rail, night of total
eclipse, he boards at Jefferson and 12th,
wears most of the clothes he owns,
layer upon layer, the rest in a ragged,
rust-colored canvas bag. "Today
is my birthday." He smiles.
"Fifty-seven." Edges of Phoenix
glimmer in the glass and fluorescent
light, our reflections fill the window,
stars blur across sky smudged
with shifting clouds. He once
had a dog, a min-pin. "Jesus,
if I could find that kind of love again."
He shakes his head. And the moon
travels into earth's shadow.

Memorial Day at Starbucks

Starbucks has decided that the woman must be removed, her existence a violation of something which the officer writes down in his notebook, the barista simply doing her job, alerting authorities to this small woman with short dark hair sitting at the far corner of the patio, whose life fills three shopping bags on the concrete next to her chair. The woman rises as the officer approaches. Tall as a tree, dressed in blue with a badge, a gun on his hip he towers over her. "They don't want you here," he says, the blazing holiday sun slashing the afternoon like a spear aimed at the patio and the wrought-iron table where the woman has placed her red and white Arby's cup which she now reaches for as she ponders this state of things that have arisen on such a sad holiday of memorialization and intoxicated driving. The tall, skinny officer looks at her with a certain kindness because he too has known loss and loneliness, but he repeats, "They don't want you here." She slips her left arm through the handles of two shopping bags, her right through the third, fingers clasped around the Arby's cup. The officer says, "There's another coffee shop down the street, just don't ask for money." And the woman walks through the empty parking lot.

A Dive Bar Called the Bardo

They've been sitting at the bar since you were eighteen and
stolen ID got you into places like this in a Phoenix reduced
now to slivers of city, simpler and more confused than western
dreams of renewal, worn and weathered nerve ends of living
that still shimmer like the bottles of Red Stag, Mango Jack,
Bicardi, Jose Cuervo and Newcastle Brown Ale beneath the
flat screen on the wall behind the bar. The woman with the
curly blond hair at the end, the man with the white hair and
short beard, baseball cap almost to his eyes staring at hands
folded on the bar as if in prayer while a local jazz band begins
a set with a keyboard riff you think is *Rikki Don't Lose That
Number* from the time your future lay in front of you like loose
change on the bar and you could wrap your arms around the
possibilities, but the clack and ding of a pinball machine
interrupts and you realize it isn't *Rikki Don't Lose That
Number* but Horace Silver's *Song for My Father,* for all
fathers, for your own father who also sat in this bar all those
years, lost in glass after glass of Rheingold Extra Dry, Camel
butt dangling from his fingers, ashes missing the tray, head
nodding until they asked you to take him home, he too far
gone to protest, slumping into the winter night, smiling
for a second when the cold hit his face, teeth white and shiny
the only part of him not stained with sorrow and you sense
he is here amongst those who have sat for so many years
at this bar where nothing changes.

The jazz number ends and a woman in a long flowing red
blouse with black and green birds approaches the stage,
jet black hair hangs below her waist, a shaman with a
message and as she reaches for the mike the drummer begins
a slow, steady drumbeat accompanied by the crying wail
of a harmonica that reminds you of Jim Morrison's Texas

Big Beat rising out of the swamps but you are in this desert
city tonight, coming home to this dive bar you've missed
for so long and the shaman woman speaks of the world
and the country and the neighborhoods and time—time you
can't slap on your wrist, program into your cell phone.
We are here for a brief series of moments, she says. In the
spaces of the music, life's sole grace. And the goal
is the same for all—avoid descending into the abyss.

Loretta Lynn in Central Phoenix

Between sips from a Circle K cup, the woman waiting for a bus at 7th and Osborn tells me she used to look like the country singer. Back in the 60s when hippy girls sold flowers on the streets and she could still see the mountains. A beat-up Fender guitar hangs from her left shoulder. A wiry mix of matted gray-black hair falls to her waist, long curls around her aged, make-up-caked face. *"Back before too many people moved to the city,"* she says. *"People with money in their hearts."* Back when she bussed tables with Waylon Jennings at John's Green Gables on 24th Street and Thomas before they turned it into real estate offices. *"That handsome boy with the outlaw soul."* She still doesn't believe he died.

She gets a free Valley Metro pass, rides all over the city, watches people, the turn of days. On Central she switches to light rail. *"Some things are the same,"* she says. Old motels untouched by upscale and gentrification. Asphalt in the summer. Energy pounding beneath the pavement. Stories in the cracks of sidewalks and the heat of the wind. *"It's dusk that's the saddest,"* she says. *"When it's too early to sleep."*

Exit 145A

A man staggers down the white line divider of the 7th Street exit ramp, feet dancing unsteadily from one lane to the other moving in the wrong direction oblivious to vehicles heading towards him, swerving to avoid hitting him, honking horns long and hard as he continues in the glare of the desert sun, hot asphalt beneath his feet shimmering as if twinkly lights blanketed the surface of the highway, this out-of-place man in a royal blue t-shirt, white bushy hair blowing whose face I briefly catch as I pass him and leave the interstate, then pull over and call Phoenix PD to report the situation only to be informed it is not their responsibility, I should call Maricopa County Sheriff's Office because this man on the interstate is within their scope and I am put on hold while the voice coming through my iPhone searches for their number and no they cannot connect me and when I do reach Maricopa County Sheriff's Office I learn the man walking towards disaster does not fall within their mandate either and I should speak with DPS whose number I look up quickly as the MCSO voice is still speaking and call immediately after hanging up but DPS is also the wrong agency and I am directed to Highway Patrol who finally takes down the information as this disoriented man approaches the crush of speeding metal and chrome in the concrete canyon that slices through our gentrified city of fissures and fragile veneers that no longer has space for him or time for his delays and detours, the lines he straddles, his thresholds, misdirections, the precipices he continually confronts, a city at once cognizant and unaware, a city that cannot stop as this man walks toward disaster, everything moving too fast and too slow.

Honey Crisps

I saw him most mornings at the intersection,
a freeway frontage road and city street
his wavy blond-gray hair in a neat ponytail,
blue eyes clear and sharp, his possessions
neatly stacked in a utility cart with two baskets.
Morning sun bounced off metal and chrome
as vehicles waited for a green light, sometimes
we chatted about the traffic, the weather.
I'd give him money. *God bless,* he'd say
and I would say *Have a nice day.*

When summer heat arrived, I asked if he needed
water, he shook his head and pointed to an 8-pack
of Aquafina in the bottom basket, a towel
and shirt folded on top. One morning, he asked
if I liked apples. I nodded. He reached into a backpack
in his cart and passed me two perfect honey crisps
red flush, gold-yellow streaks, radiant with shine.

A Sonoran Desert City

I walk before sunrise through squared-off landscapes
of suburbia, for a while it seems possible
not to think of the dry snarl of heat, the savagery
of manicured lawns, the men and women with bibles
and laws.

Sun bursts through to streets of retreating
liberties hanging by tattered threads, tents
of the unhoused, bus stops as hollow shelter.
We have failed in fatal ways, the vortex
of *civilization* surrounded by sham
choices.

And the desert echoes, exhausted and
endangered. Perhaps the project of humanity
has outlived itself, is winding down.
Perhaps we should give the world back
to the birds and fireflies, the gray wolves
and pygmy owls, the jaguars. Perhaps
we were never the best idea.

Backsplash

The way the copper-colored backsplash in your kitchen curls
and pulls away from drywall seems almost sudden though
steam and heat have risen off the stovetop for many years of
holiday dinners, pots filled with turnips, vegetables, potatoes
to be mashed, gravy bubbling with turkey drippings and at
other times everyday-cooking—water boiled for pasta or soup
and always your cast-iron teapot shot mist into the air from its
spout, so many cups of Sencha green tea sipped as you read
newspapers, imagined poetry, too busy to notice the peel of
time inching, then racing—and how your popcorn ceiling once
white as the first communion dress your mom made you on her
Singer sewing machine has dulled and discolored like dirty snow
melted and refrozen during prolonged winters of dying dark
in the cities of your childhood, leaks now when monsoons crash
into the desert sprawl never bringing enough rain to defeat
the drought or quench your own thirst and you dream of a sharp
tool to scrape the bumpy asbestos-filled stucco that will rain
down powdery fragments of poison as you shave the surface
smooth, paint it over flat and shiny, bright like a new sky
for your life, all the surly old pieces scattered on the floor
to be swept away.

Lead Me Home

The traffic signal at the railroad tracks
on Southern Avenue turns red, dusk falls
on the city, quiet this Thanksgiving
the air gentle, few cars on the road.
A man pushes a shopping cart across the street
slowly, it is piled high with his belongings,
covered in a white sheet, behind him
another man with a similar cart
on this day of gratitude, abundance
and palpable loneliness.

North from the railroad crossing an encampment
of tents. Several people follow the two men
with shopping carts, a small procession of humanity
in this city, in these times of affluence
and crushing disparity.

Lead Me Home is the name of a 39-minute documentary on unhoused human beings directed by Jon Shenk and Pedro Kos.

Morning Rush Hour at Southern
and the 101/Price Freeway

This morning West Mary wears a smile on sunbaked lips
strands of brown hair poking from a Cardinals' baseball cap

worn backwards like a statement on this parched city
of entrances and exits, human beings crossed by directions

not charted on maps or GPS, scale and distance unanchored
she treks through traffic paused for a signal

in this place of junctures and sprawl, blind land
of growth and wealth, pain and drought

I pass her a five-dollar bill and she says *God bless*
walks across three lanes of anxious vehicles

to the sidewalk in front of an abandoned Hampton Inn
backpacks and shopping carts in the parking lot

and specters of migrant children snatched
from paperless parents—god bless

The Land

To the Wild

Sitting near the edge of this red and gold escarpment that juts
over the creek below, I gaze at your splendor far from
billboards and illusions of self-importance, know that I will
carry you with me always, call upon this moment of
stillness as the sprawl of civilization overwhelms I will
conjure your rugged peaks, your canyons and creeks,
junipers and cottonwoods, sycamores, feel my feet traverse
your ground, the inclines and descents always with trust
that you will let me pass safely, keep me steady, and respect
because you have welcomed me to breathe with you, to forge
a bond, a promise for each to preserve the other in the face
of encroachment, tattered truths and noise that ensures we
never understand silence.

>May your wildness thrive
>despite sins of human greed
>may you never surrender.

Haibun is a poetic form that combines a prose poem and Haiku. It was popularized in the 17th century by Japanese poet, Matsuo Basho.

Salvation

When it comes I wonder how long the wait
      patient vapor searching for substance

suspended unanchored distant from earth's
      surface and turmoil

evaporating unnoticed in atmosphere anticipating
      a single moment of attachment

in eternal sky and uncounted time
      weightless as breath

transformed at last into heavy cloud
      water falling as relief

on roads and rooftops tents encampments
      along the city's canals and dry riverbeds

droplets like uncut diamonds clinging to windows
      reminders of the magnificence

of connections gracing us with scents of renewal
      on parched days when we grasp

Heat

Hear its silent intensity
it has no sympathy
intangible
invisible scorching air
permeates every pore
provokes
we are small particles
it could kill us
but for this moment,
exhale
slowly, let it flow
through your veins
ride it like the wind
it is part of you
you a part of it

Gray Wolves

I am sorry we didn't pay attention
to the politician who cradles papers
and rationalizations for the end
of your protection.

I am sorry we didn't listen when the philosopher
said to look into your eyes is to see our souls
we stood so close to fake gods we never imagined
your blood could taste the same as our own.

Please keep roaming crossing sandy soils
of the Chihuahuan and Sonoran surviving
with the wild horses that can't be broken,
the damaged sons and daughters in strength
and stillness fragile like the flame of a candle
before the violent breath of policy.

The Sonoran

Breathe slow and deep, make peace
with this harsh and seductive
landscape hear in its silence Whitman's
deep wisdom provoked from the soul
grasp the intensity the scratch of arid air
in your throat sometimes our world
is devastating and impossible this is therapy,
raw bleached-out desert an unexpected sanctuary
force your eyes on shriveled red buds atop saguaros,
wilted palo verde blossoms on the ground
around your feet they remind you of color
that always returns move your body through a haze
of heat-infused light at once dull and blinding
to sparse spots of shade small reliefs imperceptible
drifts of wind on your skin you wonder
about coyotes and jack rabbits, bobcats and javelina
do they experience a breeze the way you do
and you may think of human beings who cross
vast spaces of barren tracts and survive or don't
as you hike this stark place it could bless you
with the kind of thought Nietzsche said
can only be conceived while walking

Palm Fronds

hang like frayed curtains
in my backyard ragged
shadows of yesterday's
willowy swaying stalks
barely joined to trunks
they wait for monsoon
gusts to hurl them in heaps
like slaughtered corpses
on desert afternoons
they beckon the past
tell me all they've heard
and seen that I might
write it down

Scorpions

The scorpions have come into the house
to experience my walls, the contours
of my ceiling, dark crevices
between inside and out.
They come with the heat
and the night to remind me
of the fissures.

Desert Columbine

Thank you for the desert columbine
on the hiking trail
in Strawberry all those years ago
its innocent glow like a piece
of sun flickering
through the mountain pines
the world quiet with gentle
rustles and our own footsteps.

I keep it in a quart-sized
sandwich bag dried
and preserved tiny yellow
flowers fragile like aged skin
the radiance of the young
blossom could not last, but
thank you nonetheless because
it lingers in the air and sometimes
I can see its fresh beauty and smell
the soil from which it bloomed.

Mountains

We are lost in the city where truth
hangs like memory. Take us
through the river of snakes.
Across fields of Ironwood and
Saguaro to where earth demands
more space, pushes through its own skin,
rises in jagged peaks, under shafts
of sun and shimmer of sky.
We can forget for a moment
our 10,000 things and age of lies,
as holy wind passes through our veins.
We are not the answer.
Let us listen to the mountains.

About the Author

Roxanne Doty is a writer of fiction, poetry, and nonfiction. She grew up in Huntington, New York; Kansas City, Missouri and Nashville, Tennessee. She recently retired from Arizona State University where she taught in the School of Politics and Global Studies and published non-fiction for thirty years.

Her first novel, *Out Stealing Water* (Regal House Publishing), was published in September 2022. Her poems have appeared in *New Verse News, Third Wednesday, Unstrung, Espacio Fronterizo, Ocotillo Review,* and elsewhere. Her short fiction has appeared in *Superstition Review, Ocotillo Review, Lascaux Review, Journal of Microliterature, Soundings Review,* and *The Baltimore Review* among other journals. Her short story, "Turbulence," was nominated for a Pushcart Prize by the editor of *Ocotillo Review* in 2019. She currently lives in Phoenix, Arizona.

www.ingramcontent.com/pod-product-compliance
Lightning Source LLC
Chambersburg PA
CBHW031205160426
43193CB00008B/515